Amazing Animals
Lions

Please visit our web site at www.garethstevens.com
For a free catalog describing our list of high-quality books, call 1-800-542-2595 (USA) or 1-800-387-3178 (Canada).
Our fax: 1-877-542-2596

Library of Congress Cataloging-in-Publication Data

Albee, Sarah.
    Lions / by Sarah Albee.
        p. cm. — (Amazing animals)
        Originally published: Pleasantville, NY: Reader's Digest Young Families, copyright 2006.
    Includes bibliographical references and index.
    ISBN-10: 0-8368-9121-X   ISBN-13: 978-0-8368-9121-8 (lib. bdg.)
    ISBN-10: 1-4339-2125-1   ISBN-13: 978-1-4339-2125-4 (soft cover)
    1. Lions—Juvenile literature. I. Title.
    QL737.C23A399 2009
    599.757—dc22   2009003927

This edition first published in 2010 by
Gareth Stevens Publishing
A Weekly Reader® Company
1 Reader's Digest Road
Pleasantville, NY 10570-7000 USA

This edition copyright © 2010 by Gareth Stevens, Inc. Original edition copyright © 2006 by Reader's Digest Young Families, Pleasantville, NY 10570

Executive Managing Editor: Lisa M. Herrington
Senior Editor: Brian Fitzgerald
Senior Designer: Keith Plechaty

Art Direction and Page Production: The Design Lab/Kathleen Petelinsek and Gregory Lindholm
Consultant: Robert E. Budliger (Retired), NY State Department of Environmental Conservation
Spot art: Virginijus Poshkus

Photo Credits
Front cover: Photodisc by Getty Images; title page: Nova Development Corporation; contents: Dynamic Graphics, Inc.; pages 6–7: Dynamic Graphics, Inc.; page 8: IT Stock; page 9: Nova Development Corporation; page 10: Dynamic Graphics, Inc.; page 11: IT Stock; page 12: Corel Professional Photos; page 13 (left): Nova Development Corporation; page 13 (right): Photodisc by Getty Images; pages 14–15: Dynamic Graphics, Inc.; page 16 (main): Corbis Corporation; page 16 (inset): Corel Professional Photos; page 17: Photodisc; page 18: Corbis Corporation; page 19: Corel Professional Photos; page 20: Corbis Corporation; page 21: Corbis Corporation; pages 22–23: Brand X Pictures; page 24: Photodisc by Getty Images; page 25: Nova Development Corporation; page 26: Nova Development Corporation; page 27: IT Stock; page 28: IT Stock; page 29: Nova Development Corporation; pages 30–31: Photodisc by Getty Images; page 32: Digital Vision; page 35: Photodisc by Getty Images; page 36: Dynamic Graphics, Inc.; pages 38–39: Shutterstock/Til Vogt; page 40: Photodisc by Getty Images; page 43: Dynamic Graphics, Inc.; pages 44–45: Digital Vision; page 46: Nova Development Corporation; back cover: Nova Development Corporation.

Printed in the United States of America

1 2 3 4 5 6 7 8 9 13 12 11 10 09

Amazing Animals
Lions

By Sarah Albee

Gareth Stevens
Publishing

Contents

Chapter 1
A Lion's Life

On a hot, windy day, a group of lions sits in the sun-baked grass of a wide-open African plain. But one lion creeps away from the rest. She is looking for a safe place to have her babies.

The mother lion gives birth to two babies. They are tiny, blind, and helpless, completely dependent on their mother. They each weigh just about 3 pounds (1 kilogram)—less than a bag of flour. It will be three weeks before they start to walk. In the meantime, their mother feeds them. She keeps them safe from hungry hyenas and leopards by moving them to different hiding places.

After a few weeks, the mother lion decides it is time for the **cubs** to meet their father. He and their uncle are the only adult males in the group.

Wild Words

A group of lions living together is called a **pride**.

A few months pass. Early one morning, the cubs kiss their mother good-bye. She and the other females are getting ready to go off to hunt. The cubs' aunt stays behind to watch all the little cubs in the pride.

A few hours later, the hunters return. They have not brought back any food. Their hunt was unsuccessful. They will try again tonight.

Just as she is about to lie down and rest with her cubs, the mother lion leaps to her feet and growls. She has heard a roar nearby! She knows that male lions from outside her pride may try to take it over. While her cubs hide, she and the other adult females roar fiercely at the stranger. The cubs' father gets ready to do battle. Then, the stranger changes his mind about attacking. He runs away. The pride is safe!

Do Cubs Hunt?

Cubs start going with their mothers on hunts when they are nearly a year old. They remain dependent on their mothers and other lions for food until they are about two years old.

Cub Care

Lions do not leave their cubs alone and unprotected. If something happens to a mother lion, other females in the pride adopt her cubs.

After eating a big
meal, lions often
relax in the shade.

That evening, the cubs' mother goes hunting again. This time, she and the other hunters manage to kill a large animal. The pride eats well.

After the lions eat, they flop down under a group of trees. It is time for a long nap.

As the years pass, the cubs grow up quickly. The male cub starts to grow a **mane**. Soon it will be time for him to leave the pride to find his own pride and mate. The female cub will stay in the pride with her mother and other female relatives for the rest of her life.

The Body of a Lion

Listen to This!

Lions can turn their ears in different directions to hear sounds from all around. They can hear an animal that is 1 mile (1.6 kilometers) away!

Lions are the only big cats with males and females that look different from each other.

Big Cats, Small Cats

If you have a pet cat, you've probably noticed some interesting things about it. It has excellent eyesight and hearing. It moves gracefully—whether it is walking, running, or leaping. It uses its long tail for balance. Your cat often **grooms** its fur with its tongue. Also, it sleeps or rests a lot.

Now imagine a cat that does all these things. But this cat weighs 500 pounds (227 kg), is 8 feet (244 centimeters) long from nose to tail, and has a big mane. It is a male lion. It is a **mammal**, just like your pet cat.

Female lions do not have manes, and they are smaller than the males. They are about 5 feet long (152 cm) and weigh about 300 pounds (136 kg).

Do Lions Purr?

Lions can purr, but they don't do it often. A pet cat can purr while it breathes in and out. However, lions purr only when they exhale.

Glorious Manes

At age two or three, a male lion starts to grow a mane. It is fully grown when the lion is about five years old. The color ranges from pale yellow to black. The mane gets darker with age.

Some adult male lions have bigger manes than others. A large mane seems to be a status symbol. It gives its owner certain privileges and benefits. For instance, scientists have observed that the lion with the largest mane gets to eat first. Also, a lion that is getting ready to attack another lion often backs away if the opponent has a larger mane.

Manes may look heavy, but they are mostly fluff. A mane can protect a lion's head and neck from bites and scratches during fights with other lions.

Baby Teeth

Like human children, lion cubs lose their baby teeth. Their permanent teeth grow in when the cubs are about two years old. Some teeth can be as long as 2 inches (5 cm), about the length of your pinkie. An adult lion has 30 teeth.

Padded Paws

Lions have thick padding on the bottoms of their paws. These special pads help lions move quietly. The pads prevent lions from skidding on slippery surfaces, just like your sneakers help you.

Adult male lions are the only cats with manes.

Copy Cat

Have you ever watched someone else yawn and then started to yawn yourself? The same thing happens with lions. Yawning, grooming, and roaring all seem to be contagious among lions. If one does it, it sets off a wave across the pride.

Lions can leap an amazing distance in one bound—as far as 35 feet (11 meters)! Their strong muscles also allow them to capture an animal three times their size.

Lions in Action

Lions can run, jump, pounce, climb trees—and even swim if they have to. Like other cats, their backs are flexible. This flexibility, combined with their powerful leg muscles, lets lions leap high in the air and land safely.

Similar to other cats, lions have excellent vision and hearing. Lions can see in the dark, and their widely spaced eyes let them see to the sides.

Cool Cats

Lions like to rest during the day, when the sun is hottest. Young lions climb trees to take advantage of cooling breezes. Older, bigger lions look for a shady spot under trees. Sometimes, lions lie on their backs to allow the air to cool their undersides.

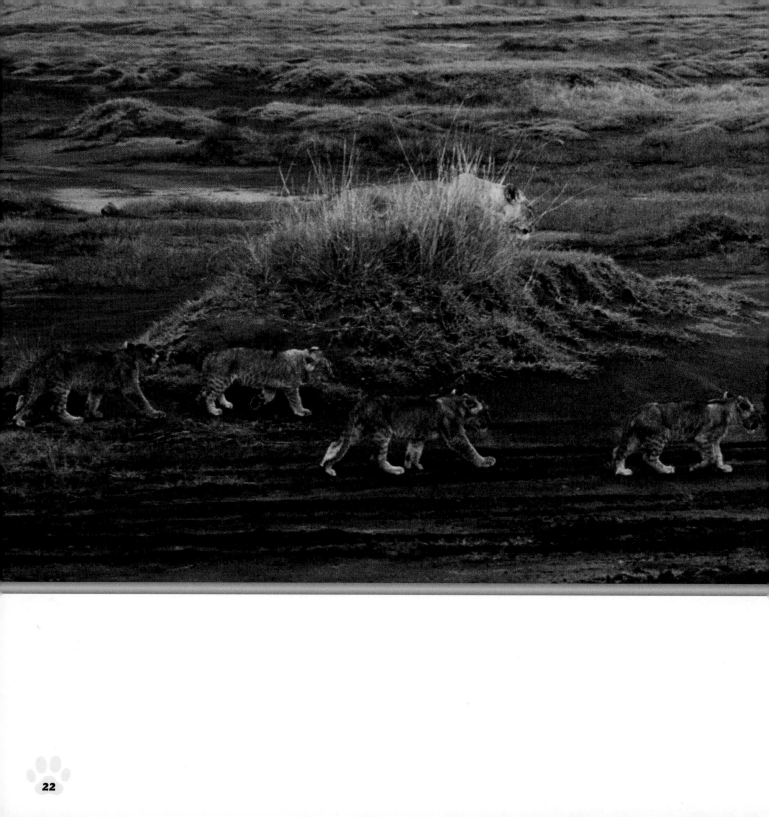

Chapter 3
Lion Families

Lion Cooperation

Lions are the only members of the cat **species** that work together to raise their young and to hunt for food.

Mothers, daughters, sisters, and female cousins usually live in the same pride their whole lives. Males stay for only a few years.

A Matter of Pride

A pride can include as many as 40 lions, but big prides often separate into smaller groups. A pride usually consists of two to 18 females and their cubs, as well as one to seven males, with one male as chief. Other males may challenge the chief lion, which is overthrown every three years or so.

The adult females in the group care for the cubs, find water, decide where the group will sleep, and hunt for food. If a mother dies, other females will adopt her cubs.

When male cubs reach the age of about two or three, they are ready to leave the pride. For a time, they travel without a pride, sometimes in pairs, hunting on their own. Two brothers or male cousins will often remain together for life. When they are fully grown, they try to take control of another pride.

Wild Words

In Africa, the word for *lion* in Swahili is **simba**. Simba also means "strong" and "king."

Heads and Tails

How do lions announce their presence to others? One good way is to roar! Lions roar to let other lions of their pride know where they are. Males also roar to warn rivals to stay away from their **territory**. A pride's territory covers about 40 to 50 square miles (104 to 129 sq km). This is about the same size as the city of Boston.

Another way lions warn other animals to stay away is by marking their territory. Male lions mark their territory with a combination of urine and scent. The scent is made by special glands at the base of their tails. Lions put their scent at nose-level, so that other lions can easily detect the odor. They also scratch marks on trees and other places as warnings.

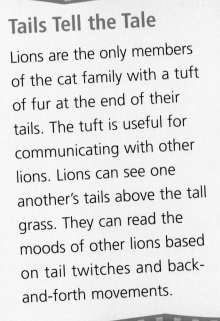

Tails Tell the Tale

Lions are the only members of the cat family with a tuft of fur at the end of their tails. The tuft is useful for communicating with other lions. Lions can see one another's tails above the tall grass. They can read the moods of other lions based on tail twitches and back-and-forth movements.

Lions have very expressive faces. They use their facial expressions, as well as their bodies, to communicate. Lions commonly greet one another by head-rubbing and grooming.

The roar of a lion can sometimes be heard 5 miles (8 km) away.

Lion cubs love to play. Like human kids, they try to get their parents' attention any way they can.

Playtime

Lion cubs spend a great deal of time playing together. They play-fight, chase one another, and wrestle. Adults occasionally join in. A mother will flick her tail, allowing the cubs to pounce on it. Much of cubs' play imitates skills they will use as adults, such as stalking and pouncing. Playing is an important way for cubs to bond with one another. Often, they remain lifelong companions.

Keeping Clean

Lions are careful groomers. They keep their front paws, manes, and chests clean with their rough tongues. Lions groom themselves and one another. Grooming other lions reinforces social bonds. It is also more thorough. A lion grooming itself licks in the same direction the fur grows. Another lion can lick in the opposite direction.

Chapter 4
King of the Beasts

Leaping Lions

Lions are able to sprint as fast as 35 miles (56 km) per hour for short distances. Most of the animals they chase can run a lot faster than that. So lions quietly creep up close to their **prey**—within 20 or 30 feet (6 or 9 m). Then they dash out and leap onto their victims to try to overpower them.

A lion chasing down prey can run the length of a football field in 6 seconds.

Going on the Hunt

In order to survive, lions spend a lot of their waking time hunting for food. Lions are **carnivores**, which means they eat other animals. Lions eat impalas, zebra, gazelles, buffalo, giraffes, wildebeest, antelope, wild boars, and even young hippopotamuses. During hard times, lions eat practically anything—fish, snakes, fruit, and even insects.

Female lions are smaller and faster than male lions. So they are the ones that most often do the hunting for the pride. Over time, lions have learned that they are more successful at catching very large prey when they hunt together. Usually one group of lions circles the prey and then stops in front of it. Meanwhile, another group of lions scares the prey from behind, forcing it to run right into the first group of lions.

Young male lions, alone or in pairs, also hunt. The chief male may join a hunt. Sometimes, his greater size and strength are needed to bring down an animal much bigger than the females.

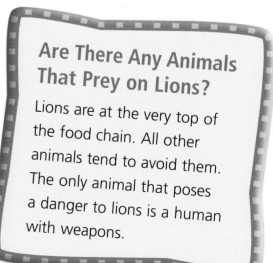

Are There Any Animals That Prey on Lions?

Lions are at the very top of the food chain. All other animals tend to avoid them. The only animal that poses a danger to lions is a human with weapons.

Table Manners

Lion hunts are often unsuccessful. If they have not caught their prey after a short chase, the lions give up. They are too tired to continue.

Sometimes, it's easier to take another animal's food. When lions hear the sound of hyenas, wild dogs, or other large cats eating, they know where they can get a fast meal. Few animals are foolish enough to protest when hungry lions show up to take their dinner.

Animals that have died are also food for lions. When lions see vultures circling in the air, it is a signal that a **carcass** is available.

Females generally bring down prey. But the males tend to eat first. Occasionally, the females can take a few bites before the males chase them away. When the male lions are finished eating, the females eat their fill. Then, the cubs and young lions are allowed to eat. Some aggressive cubs sneak in and eat with the males, but most of the pride will wait their turn.

An adult male lion can eat as much as 90 pounds (40 kg) of meat in one meal.

Lions do a lot of resting and sleeping—as much as 20 hours in a 24-hour day.

Big Cat Naps

Lions do most of their hunting at night or very early in the morning. The air is cooler then. When they find food, lions gorge themselves. They eat as much as they can and then some more. They know from experience that it might be several days before they have another successful hunt and are able to eat again.

Lions often like to take a nap after eating a large meal. Resting is a good way for lions to conserve energy. Hunting is hard work!

Other animals often graze close to resting or sleeping lions and don't seem at all frightened or concerned. They appear to understand that lions resting out in the open pose no danger to them.

Always Room for Seconds!

Lions have expandable stomachs that stretch, allowing lions to eat huge amounts of food at one time. They may then go three or four days without eating again.

Chapter 5
Lions in the World

Lion Land

Most lion **habitats** are wooded areas with open spaces. Lions are able to survive in extreme **drought** conditions. They can even live in deserts.

Wild Words

Many lions live on **savannas**. A savanna is a hot grassland area with scattered trees. It has two seasons—a long, dry one and a short one with very heavy rains. During the dry season, the grass dries out and turns golden brown.

Lions are the light brown color of sun-dried grass. Their color helps them blend into their surroundings and sneak up on their prey.

Where Lions Live

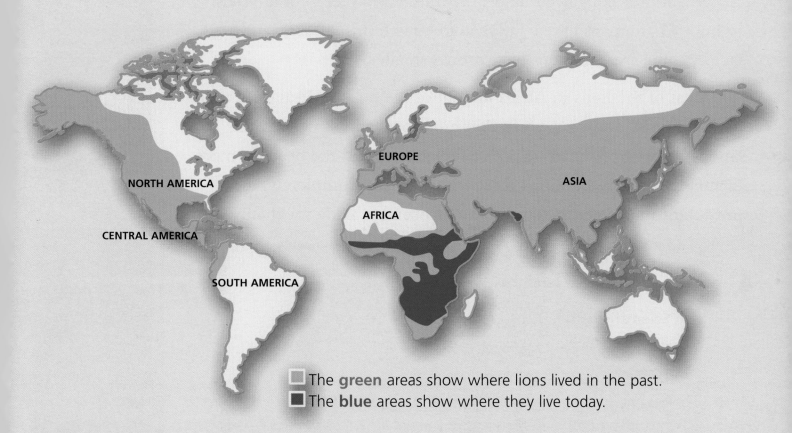

NORTH AMERICA

CENTRAL AMERICA

SOUTH AMERICA

EUROPE

AFRICA

ASIA

☐ The **green** areas show where lions lived in the past.
☒ The **blue** areas show where they live today.

Thousands of years ago, lions lived on the continents in Europe, Asia, and the Americas. However, due to changes in climate, hunting by humans, and the growth of farms and cities, the habitat of lions has decreased enormously. So has the number of lions. Today, almost all the lions on Earth live in Africa. Scientists are not sure exactly how many lions live in Africa. They estimate that there are fewer than 50,000 lions there. A few hundred lions live in India.

The Future of Lions

To survive, lions need land to roam on and plenty of animals to hunt. As humans have continued to build farms, houses, and factories, the areas for lions have grown smaller.

Most of the lions in Africa and all of the lions in India live in national parks and **preserves** that are protected. Now, even this land is being threatened by population growth and the need for more farmland. To protect lions from disappearing completely, it is important to protect the land that has been set aside for them.

Fast Facts About Lions

Scientific name	*Panthera leo*
Class	Mammals
Order	Carnivora
Size (not including tail)	Males: about 8 feet (244 cm) in length Females: about 5 feet (152 cm) in length
Weight	Males: up to 500 pounds (227 kg) Females: up to 300 pounds (136 kg)
Life span	About 15 years in the wild About 30 years in captivity
Habitat	Grasslands and open, wooded areas
Top speed	35 miles (56 km) per hour in short bursts

The Cat Family

All cats—including lions and your pet house cat—belong to the same scientific family, called *Felidae*. Lions, tigers, leopards, and jaguars are even more closely related to one another. They are from the **genus** called *Panthera*.

You Can Help!

Become a member of a **conservation** group that works to protect the habitats of lions. It may even be your local zoo.

Glossary

carcass—the body of a dead animal

carnivore—a meat-eating animal

conservation—the protection and preservation of land, animals, plants, and other natural resources

cub—a young meat-eating mammal

drought—a long period of time without rain

ecosystem—all the living and nonliving things in a certain environment

genus—a large category of related plants or animals consisting of smaller groups (species) of closely related plants or animals

groom—to clean the fur, skin, or feathers of an animal

habitat—the natural environment where an animal or a plant lives

mammal—a kind of animal with a backbone and hair on its body; it drinks milk from its mother when it is born

mane—long hair on the head or neck of an animal

predator—an animal that hunts and eats other animals to survive

preserve—an area where plants and animals are protected

prey—animals that are hunted by other animals for food

pride—a group of lions that live together

savanna—a flat grassland area with scattered trees in a hot region of the world

simba—the Swahili word for "lion," "strong," and "king"

species—a group of living things that are the same in many ways

territory—an area of land that an animal considers to be its own and will fight to defend

Lions: Show What You Know

How much have you learned about lions? Grab a piece of paper and a pencil and write your answers down.

1. What is another name for a group of lions living together?

2. How much does a newborn lion cub weigh?

3. How many teeth does an adult lion have?

4. When a group of lions begins a feast, which lions eat first?

5. What is the Swahili word for *lion*?

6. What is the purpose of the tuft of fur at the end of a lion's tail?

7. Why do females do most of the hunting for a group of lions?

8. At what age do cubs start helping their mothers with hunting?

9. What is the only animal posing a danger to lions?

10. What is a lion's top speed when sprinting for short distances?

1. A pride 2. About 3 pounds (1 kg) 3. 30 4. The males 5. Simba 6. It is used to communicate with other lions. 7. They are smaller and faster than the males. 8. At about one year old 9. A human with weapons 10. 35 miles per hour (56 kph)

For More Information

Books

Hanel, Rachael. *Lions* (Living Wild). Mankato, MN: Creative Education, 2008.

Joubert, Dereck, and Beverly Joubert. *Face to Face With Lions* (Face to Face With Animals). Washington, DC: National Geographic Children's Books, 2008.

Lockwood, Sophie. *Lions* (The World of Mammals). Mankato, MN: The Child's World, 2008.

Web Sites

Animal Planet: Lion

http://animal.discovery.com/mammals/lion

Check out videos and blogs, and take a quiz to test your knowledge of the king of the jungle.

National Geographic Kids: Lions

http://kids.nationalgeographic.com/Animals/CreatureFeature/Lion

Get quick facts, see videos and photos, and learn about lions at the Oakland Zoo.

Index